Finding Muchness

How to add more life to life

_____

Written by Kobi Yamada
Illustrated by Charles Santoso

You are bursting with promise, potential, and possibility.
You have so much to give, and so much to offer.

This is your life. This is your time.

This is your chance to do everything you've wanted to do.

Live bravely, care deeply, share freely. Get the most out
of each shining moment. Fill your life with love and stuff
your days with wonder. Because when you willingly throw
yourself into everything you do, that's when you come alive—
that's when the magic sparks.

Dream until it's true.
Believing it's possible is an
essential part of making it so.

Take the biggest step you can
toward what you want.
Then, from there, take another step.

If you want something new,
try something new.
Create what you wish existed.

Our greatest obstacles are often ourselves.
If you think you can't, you probably won't.
But if you think you can, you most likely will.

Lose yourself in what you love.
Find yourself there too.

If in doubt, love more.
The heart is much like a balloon:
the fuller it becomes,
the more it wants to fly.

It isn't, it isn't, it isn't... until it is.
Determination creates its own possibilities.

How you do one thing is how you do everything.
And anything worth doing is worth doing well.

Effort is a path to achievement, and more importantly, to improvement. You can do whatever you are willing to practice.

Worrying uses your imagination to
create things you don't want. And your
mind will believe what you feed it.
So feed it hope. Feed it love. Feed it truth.

Don't ever give up.
Especially on yourself.

We often regret what we didn't do
much more than what we did.
Risk caring deeply. Risk looking foolish.
Choose courage over comfort.

Stand up for what you believe, even if your legs are shaky.
Being brave and being afraid often occur at the same time.

Remember to be gentle with yourself.
Deep breaths are like little love notes to your body.

Be generous. Some of the best things
you'll ever get are what you give.

Know the value of being there for someone else.
Doing good and feeling good are connected.

Be kind to everything that lives.

Gratitude is the secret to happiness.
When you are grateful, you find
so much more to be grateful for.

Don't wait for things to be simpler, easier, or better. Life will always be complicated. Learn to be happy now. And know that no matter the time or day, it will always be now.

Life is a playground.
Don't forget to play.

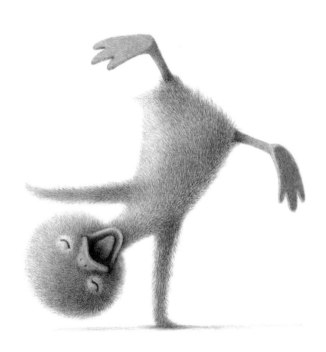

Add to the world's wonder.

Remember that you have so much within you and so many gifts to share. Your life can be everything you've hoped for... and much, much more.

Written by: Kobi Yamada
Illustrated by: Charles Santoso
Edited by: Kristin Eade
Art Directed by: Justine Edge

Library of Congress Control Number: 2020944695 | ISBN: 978-1-970147-43-8

2nd printing. Printed in China with soy inks on FSC®-Mix certified paper.

Create meaningful moments with gifts that inspire.

CONNECT WITH US
live-inspired.com | sayhello@compendiuminc.com

@compendiumliveinspired
#compendiumliveinspired

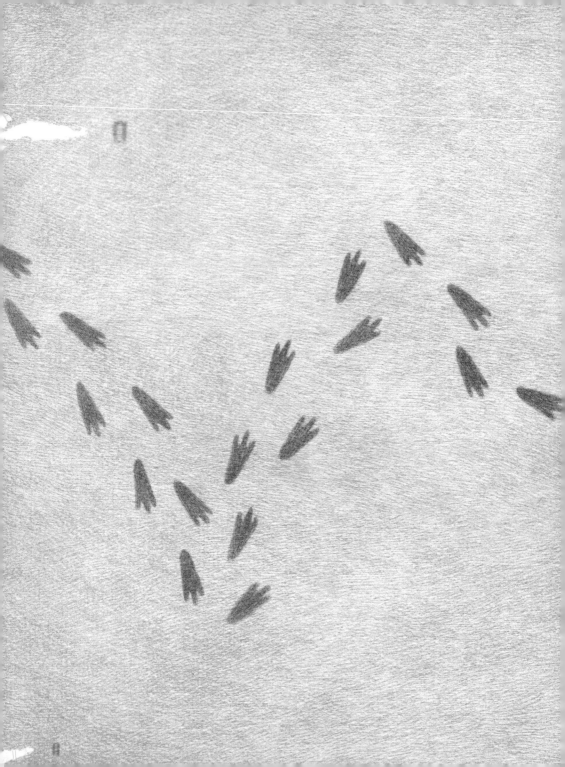